Discover and Recover

Antoinette Murphy

© 2023 Antoinette Murphy
antoinettemurphy773@aol.com

Freedom Publishing
49 Kingmere, South Terrace
Littlehampton, BN17 5LD, United Kingdom
www.freedompublishing.net

ISBN: 978-1-908154-67-5

British Library Cataloguing in Publication Data. A catalogue record for this book is available from the British Library

Formatted by Freedom Publishing
Cover by Esther Kotecha, EKDesign
Printed in the United Kingdom

Contents

Endorsements

I have known Antoinette for many years and am honoured to write an endorsement for her book.

This book is very real, it is raw, with Antoinette being completely honest about some of the darker times in her life. She has chosen to make herself completely vulnerable in order to impress upon you where God has brought her to. If you recognise yourself in any part of her story it will encourage and strengthen you - simply because what God has done for my friend, He can do for any one of us. There are times of reflection contained herein; be kind to yourself and allow time to sit with God and let Him bring healing and wholeness to those hurting places. He is after all, the 'Way maker, Miracle worker, Promise keeper and the Light in the darkness.'

Rev. Bill Hoggard and Mrs Nola Hoggard
Retired church pastors

For too long Christians have buried their heads and hearts in the sand, with the belief that "Once they are saved, they are healed and will not have any problems." In 'Discover and Recover', Antoinette explores issues that are far too often overlooked in the church. Antoinette writes from the heart and from a place of experience, in her writing and honesty she opens herself up and makes herself very vulnerable. The way she intersperses her poetry with scriptures is inspired. I recommend this book to you.

Jacqui Bimson
Senior Pastor at Preston Prophetic Centre

Antoinette's honest and revealing book will bring you so much closer to the reality of God, His love, faithfulness and truth. This book has not come easily. Through her own journey from darkness to light, through a lot of 'discovering and recovering', she has encountered the reality and goodness of God, the truth of His word and the healing she so desperately needed, that only He can bring.

This book is designed to encourage you to search out the reality of God and His kingdom, love, faithfulness and truth for yourself. It has been my absolute privilege and pleasure to have been part of Antoinette's journey into freedom and wholeness.

Lasona Moore
Retired Prison Chaplain and current Senior Leader of
'Darkness to Light Ministries'

Foreword

This book is written and sent to you from our wonderful Father in heaven. He is much better than your dad could ever be.

He is PERFECT.

He knows how life has been for you in every way, time and circumstance; He knows you through and through and through. His desire is for you to be whole again, all the areas of brokenness to be put back together perfectly by Him. To discover the REAL, AUTHENTIC you and to know that He has carried you when you were unaware of Him.

Nothing can separate you from His unfailing love!

He knows what you are thinking at this very moment and your response to Him.

He will never leave you, let you down, forget or ignore you!

You are extremely precious to Him!

He knows your opinions, things that make you tick, how you roll and the things that make you sick!

He does not miss a trick!

Your journey through life is immensely personal, known only by you and Him!

I pray as you read these pages...

"That you may come to know [practically, through experience for yourselves] the love of Christ, which far surpasses mere knowledge [without experience]; that you may be filled [through your inmost being] unto all the fullness of God [may have the richest measure of the divine presence; and become a body wholly filled and flooded with God Himself]." (Ephesians 3:19)

The poems throughout this book are written from personal life experiences and testimonies and are conversations between myself and the Lord. They are written as encouragements for you to retrieve the very personal treasures He has in store for you. It has taken me years to understand and accept my purposes in life through a lot of 'Discovering and Recovering.'

Enjoy reading.... I emphasise again, your life is an extremely personal one in relationship with our wonderful Father, Jesus and the Holy Spirit as they all work together, agreeing with one another in total unity in every way at all times!

Be blessed, very blessed!

The Eternal Invitation

God invites each and every one of us to know Him as He really is. This is what He says...

Dear (Put your name in),

I am inviting you to come further into the wonderful plans I have planned for you from before the beginning of time. In My kingdom of love, joy and peace is everything you need. I have the BEST things here for you here, all the time.

Will you come to My banquet? There is everything here for us to enjoy together. There is no fear in love; perfect love drives out fear. (1 John 4:18)

There is joy, laughter, peace and total harmony here. You will know that you're fully understood, cherished, adored, and that I am never disappointed in you, ever!

I love to hear your voice, in fact I love your company all together. I know your weaknesses, strengths, frustrations, your real questions about how life has been for you.

Welcome! You do not have to rush in, come at your own pace; I understand your reservations. I know you need to understand and trust Me, stage by stage, one step at a time.

There are things that I will reveal to you that will cause you to be truly alive. Yes, you are intimately known by Me! My Son has done EVERYTHING for you at the cross so you can experience true love, total acceptance; there is true, authentic, personal and total healing for you in every aspect of your life.

All the consequences and the effects of being sinned against, ignored, bullied, neglected, abused, rejected, yes even by your own family, alongside your own sin, are dealt with at the cross - the death and resurrection of My Son. The whole of Isaiah's prophecy in chapter 53 (NIV) was fulfilled there.

"Surely He took up our pain and bore our suffering, yet we considered Him punished by God, stricken by Him, and afflicted."

But He was pierced for our transgressions, He was crushed for our iniquities; the punishment that brought us peace was upon Him, and by His wounds we are healed. We all, like sheep have gone astray, each of us has turned to our own way; and the LORD has laid on Him the iniquity of us all.

He was oppressed and afflicted, yet He did not open His mouth; He was led like a lamb to the slaughter, as a sheep before its shearers is silent, so He did not open His mouth; By oppression and judgement He was taken away. Yet who of His generation protested? For He was cut off from the land of the living; For the transgression of My people He was punished. He was assigned a grave with the wicked and with the rich in His death, although He had done no violence, nor was there any deceit in His mouth. Yet it was the LORD's will to crush Him and cause Him to suffer, and though the LORD makes His life an offering for sin, He will see His offspring and prolong his days, and the will of the LORD will prosper in his hand." (Isaiah 53:4-10 NIV)

I want nothing, absolutely nothing to come between us because "Every dividing wall of hostility is broken down." (Ephesians 2:14)

Please trust Me, I will not force you to come; I long for you, I love you so much.

"Many waters cannot quench love!" (Song of Songs 8:7)

All you will ever get from Me is PURE, untainted love, a love which humans cannot give. I will not deceive you; I am TRUE, I believe you are too. There is nothing hidden from My sight.

"Nothing in all creation is hidden from God's sight." (Hebrews 4:13 NIV)

Can we talk together?

I am always listening, even when you don't speak out loud.

Notes

Definitions of Discover and Recover

I am starting this book with these definitions because I believe it is helpful to know that there are different meanings and aspects of discovering and recovering. The Lord wants to impact, change and bring each and every one of us into complete wholeness in deeply personal ways. Remember He knows how to do this for everyone as He knows everyone intimately.

"(Not in your own strength) for it is God Who is all the while effectually at work in you (energising and creating in you the power and desire) both to will and to work for His good pleasure and satisfaction and delight." (Philippians 2: 13)

Recently I have discovered what iniquity really is, how it almost ruined my life through my twisted, out of control, destructive behaviour, responses and reactions to traumas I experienced. I am now free from their power and influence in my life because Jesus has dispelled, nullified and destroyed their power over me!

I am sober, hopeful, free from fear and out of religion, where I depended on other things to please God instead of just responding to His love and cultivating a true personal relationship with Him.

I have recovered some of the personal treasures which belong to me which are a sound, undisturbed mind, peace in my soul, true rest, a light spirit, knowing I am totally understood, cared for and restored to joy.

I encourage you to seek the Lord in this phase of your life, your deeply personal journey with Him. What will He reveal to you? How will you respond? What will you discover? What will you recover?

Only He knows!

I can guarantee that He will do everything in His mighty power and love to do you good and bring wholeness in every area of your life!

"The LORD will perfect that which concerns me: Your mercy and loving kindness, O LORD, endure forever - forsake not the works of Your own hands." (Psalm 138:8)

Definition of Discover:

Discovery ... Find, come across, detect, dig up, ferret out, happen on, hit on, locate, track down, turn up, uncover, unearth, ascertain, determine, discern, find out, notice, perceive, realise.

Definition of Recover:

Regain possession or control of.

Return to health, recovery. Get or win back, recapture, recoup, regain, repossess, retake, retrieve, rescue, salvage, save.

Be on the mend, convalesce, get better or well, improve, pick up, rally, recuperate, revive.

Recovery, recapture, reclamation, repossession, retrieval, rescue, salvage, convalesce, improvement, recuperation.

As a believer, you need to take hold of the things which are rightfully yours. As believers, we acknowledge the reality of healing and wholeness; however, we do not really grasp the fullness of them unless we have revelation from the Holy Spirit and knowledge of God's word. This book is written to inform you of some of the riches found in Christ Jesus. You will discover many more of them too. They are endless and found only in Him!

"I pray that out of His glorious riches, He may strengthen you with power through His Spirit in your inner being, so that Christ may dwell in your hearts through faith." (Ephesians 3:16 NIV)

Notes

My Childhood

My life as it was and how I was shaped into the person I became.

As a child, I was given into the care of my nan and grandad. My mum was 19 years old when I was born. She was fearful, brought up in a Catholic school and taught by nuns who were violent and bullied her. She was also dominated by my nan, who looked after me because my mum had to work a few jobs. My dad was married (not to my mum) with two other children. All of my other siblings lived either with mum or dad. My mum was never married to my dad. She married a violent alcoholic who beat her badly and frequently smashed up the house. I witnessed this on occasions when I stayed for a weekend. My brother wet himself with fear one night before the police came to arrest his dad. One time, I was upstairs in bed and heard them shouting and screaming - the crashing, banging sounds woke me up. As I came down the stairs, halfway down one of them told me to get back up and the other told me come down. I was frozen and confused.

I remember that I loved the doll's house made from matchsticks my (adoptive) dad made for me when he was in jail. I loved visiting him there and counted the days excitedly before going. We went in a big white van. Mum told us he was in a hospital. I guess she was ashamed of him.

My youngest brother died from cot death aged 3 months old. This was extremely traumatic for mum. It led to their divorce as my stepdad, who had legally adopted me, could not cope and the violence increased.

At 10 years old, I was hit by a car and went through the windscreen. I remember lying on the road, seeing ankles around me, my yellow blanket and a wardrobe with a Dumbo sticker on it. I also remember going hysterical, screaming for my mum "I want my mum! I want my mum! I want my mum!"

She came, and I heard her arguing with my dad outside the ward in the corridor. As the nurse brushed my hair, tiny cubes of glass filled my duffle coat pockets. I was walking to the swimming baths when it happened, so the rubber cap I was wearing under my duffle coat hood had protected my skull, although it still got fractured. I was in hospital for a week with a broken leg; my shin bones were completely shattered. This meant I was unable to climb the stairs and had to eat from a chair beside the sofa, so my nan decided she could not manage to look after me any longer and I went to live with my mum and brother. When Mum put her arm around my shoulder to cuddle me, I froze, this was such an unfamiliar experience for me. Not knowing how to accept love, I became very lonely; so terrified of the dark. I often saw (in my mind's eye) horrible demons who told me I was blessed to have them in my life. This made me feel very fearful, disoriented and abandoned.

I had always wanted to ask mum if she would take me home with her and my brother. Even as a child I knew there was a 50/50 chance of her saying "No." This would have broken my little heart, so I never did ask. She took my brother home after having a cup of tea with my nan, her mum, every evening after she came from work. I would look behind the curtains in the winter to see if mum was coming, I could not wait to see her.

I longed for her to show me love. She could not, her brokenness and the consequences of trauma made her incapable of this. She did buy me sweets and left me at the bus stop daily before she went to work, then I walked to and back from school on my own. I was quite independent. However I didn't really feel connected to my mum and only have a few memories of her engaging with me as her daughter.

I met my biological dad and full blood sister for the first time when I was nine years old. I would visit my dad's home regularly. Although it was not as clean as my home, I felt a lot of love there. I really wanted to live there but I never asked. I loved seeing my biological dad and sister, I felt less alone there and loved being around a fun, happy, loving family. I felt connected and knew I belonged with them.

Those first ten years of my life were harsh. Sad, lonely, rejected, sexually abused by men in my street; one of them made me eat ice cubes and held a knife to my neck, threatening me if I told anyone about it. I was fearful, confused, shamed, angry, traumatised and easily compliable. My grandad went to the pub every night, he was often drunk and would argue with my nan. Somehow I too developed a craving for beer, wanting to down a pint while watching an advert for beer on the television. Every day in the school holidays we sat outside the pub eating crisps and drinking pop. Then we waited outside the betting shop before going home before Nan came back from work. She was a cleaner at the local hospital. We would always play in old garages and play 'Kerby', which we called 'Gutters'.

I remember at school having to watch a film called 'The Sorcerer's Apprentice.' I really felt the presence of evil and wanted to leave the room. I could not; I didn't want to make a fuss. I was scared, wishing someone would take me out. I loved being in the school play though, I was Eeyore the donkey, although I wanted to be Tigger. I was so disappointed that I couldn't be in the play when I broke my leg. The teachers wanted me to take the lead role of a cowgirl. I was in the top class throughout my school years, loving Art and English. I was shy but loved sports and was in all the sports teams. I played badminton regularly and was coached from the age of 12 as my ability, talent and potential were evident. I could have been involved in local tournaments but was too busy drinking alcohol and being promiscuous.

Every Halloween, I became absolutely terrified of witches, ghosts, and the darkness I felt around me. Bonfire night, though, was my favourite night of the year, second only to Christmas Eve. On the 6th of November I would get out the small artificial Christmas tree and start to decorate it every night until the middle of December, begging my nan to let me keep it up every evening. I would kneel at my bedside and say the Lord's Prayer every night. I had a fascination with the Bible, which was a big, gilt edged Catholic one. I sat behind the sofa reading it. A picture of John the Baptist's head on a plate scared me so much I was afraid to pick it up again. I guess I knew God was real.

Looking back, I can see that God was revealing Himself to me as I sat behind the sofa and when I prayed at night. I knew that someone was with me. I was also saved from a potentially fatal road accident when I was a child and one day as I walked with my Nan, brother and our dog at the top of a set of steps in a graveyard, they all literally fell over. I didn't and I knew that someone stopped me from falling down.

"Before I was born, the LORD called me; from my mother's womb He has spoken my name" (Isaiah 49:1 NIV)

"And I will restore or replace for you for the years that the locust has eaten." (Joel 2:25)

"The thief only comes to steal and kill and destroy; I have come that they may have life and have it to the full" (John 10:10 NIV)

"Instead of your shame, you shall have a double, twofold recompense, instead of dishonour and reproach you shall rejoice in your portion. Therefore in your land you shall possess double (what you have forfeited); everlasting joy shall be yours! For I, the LORD love justice; I hate robbery and wrong with violence or a burnt offering. And I will give your recompense in truth and I will make an everlasting covenant or league with you." (Isaiah 61:7-8)

"Because you are honoured and precious in My sight and because I love you. I will give men in return for your life and people in exchange for your life." (Isaiah 43:4)

He has seen all throughout, and He was there in every situation during your childhood. Every word that has been spoken to you and by you He has heard. He knows how your life experiences have shaped you into the person you are today.

His heart is FULL of compassion for you.

A Poem

Stares, Glares, Nightmares

Stares, glares, nightmares
Kids jumping in squares
Did anyone see what happened then?
Who knows, when I wore those scruffy clothes
someone might have I suppose.

"Yes, I saw and was appalled
You could not hear My voice at first when I called
You read My word and met Me then
Remember?

Your life has been and is in My hands
A little girl whose dreams were dashed, life crashed
"A new day." you said. Disappointment came
You were never the same.
Hope deferred makes the heart sick, but a longing fulfilled
is a tree of life
Hope is here for you now, it always has been
I will satisfy your every desire, burn in you like fire
You'll be truly alive, your purpose will be clear.

I will repay you for the years that the locusts have eaten
It's okay to seem beaten, just press on I'll bring you
through
You'll get answers to why you're here
That's certain, you'll come from behind the curtain.

I'm so proud of you, how you have come through
I am true, always here for you
Not distant or afar, closer than you know
I am happy living in you, yes well at home
I desire all of you, in ways you have no clue
Yes, stuck with the strongest of glue.

Test Me, try Me and see, you'll not be disappointed
Only anointed and truly free
I will never fail you!"

This poem was written at a Christian Healing Centre when
I was receiving healing from past traumas.

The Lord is totally committed to healing you from any and
every trauma that may have happened in your life....

Notes

Stolen Treasures

It is clear from God's word that we have an enemy who is a thief. How does he do this? He accuses us, making us feel guilt and condemnation, although because of the death and resurrection of Jesus we are deemed "Not guilty!"

The thief will use our upbringing, circumstances, ancestral iniquitous patterns of behaviour, addictions, being abused in any way, rejection, traumatic experiences, fears, being involved in martial arts, religion and false supernatural experiences (e.g., Ouija boards, Tarot cards, Horoscopes, fortune telling, palm reading, ESP (Extra Sensory Perception), dowsing etc.). He will also use false religions like Buddhism, Islam, Sikhism, Wicca, Mormonism, and the rest, or any sickness, physical, emotional, mental and spiritual. His only aim is to destroy us. However, this does not have to be the case. We can repent of any involvement in any of these things, sever our bloodlines of specific iniquities and receive forgiveness; then we can actually retrieve the things stolen from us during our lifetime.

One day a few years ago, the Lord asked me to spend the afternoon with Him. It was a few days after I had written a list of things that had been stolen from me which I wanted to get back. These were...

Dignity
Peace
Security
Acceptance
Being loved
Affirmation
Joy
Identity
Innocence
A father's love
Affection
A loving home
Feeling safe
Rest
Sleep
A purpose
Comfort
Being understood
Having a family in the same house
A reason to live
Being celebrated
Being remembered
A mother's love
Being taken seriously

As I lay on my bed, I went up into a room in the Spirit. A massive pile of all sorts of treasures and jewels was in the centre of the room touching the ceiling. I wondered if these were maybe the things on my list. I asked the Lord if this was biblical in case I thought wrongly. I looked on the floor and saw a note saying Ezekiel 22. This is what it says in verse 25... "like a roaring lion tearing the prey. They have devoured [human] life; they have taken [in their greed] treasure and precious things."

I was amazed and glad I asked the question. He said "Tell people that they can come and retrieve the things that were stolen from them; their treasures."

So, whatever treasures have been stolen from you, you can retrieve them ALL!

Make your own list if you want to... Ask Him, talk to Him. He already knows you inside out. Your whole life even. He will lead you into ALL truth... (John 16:26)

What can stop you is fear, shame, guilt and the rest. I can fully reassure you; He knows you, He is for you and not against you. Things will work out for you as you co-operate with Him, through relationship, living in and being sustained by His unfailing love.

A Poem

Trauma, Numb, Dumb

Trauma, numb, can't speak, dumb
Can't remember, recall
Want to forget it – Will it just go away?

It happened, made an impression
Lost humanity, only a possession

Who or where am I?

I'm not here, gone, dead?
Alive, trying to survive
Drugs, alcohol, the rest, does not do it I've tried
Where can I go to get that peace, release and comfort from?
Is it over for me?
No, it's a lie, because I knew you before you were born
Remember the pain, shame and scorn.
Angry, sad, in a rage?
I understand you, I am on your page

Yes, I am pure love you don't know yet
Listen, can you hear Me speaking tenderly to you?

This was written after I left my husband, feeling sad, alone, frozen and depressed. I heard His tender words which lifted me up. I sobbed my heart out to Him and was comforted by the Holy Spirit.

Maybe you can listen and write down what He is saying to you... He will speak tenderly to you too...

Notes

My Teenage Years

I don't remember much of them; they were, as you might expect, turbulent, emotional and full of bad behaviour. My mum met a man who was 18 years old; she was 32, I was 12 and my brother was 9 years old. They fell in love and were devoted to each other. I, however, felt and experienced more rejection. I did not even feel welcome in my own home. Glancing through the windows of every house I passed by, I imagined being part of that family, loved, safe, secure and able to be who I really was. Drinking cider, lager and getting drunk became normal to me. Promiscuity, low self-esteem, disruptive behaviour in school, 'being brave' by refusing to cry when I really wanted to, dismissing my need to be heard and noticed; these became my life.

Notes

A Life Changing Encounter

At 22 years old, I went to a church meeting with my brother and his girlfriend, although I did not want to. During this meeting, I heard a voice which said, "I know everything about you and I love you." I wanted to cry but, as ever, did not acknowledge my feelings; I was numb. Afterwards, I went to the pub to meet friends. I could not enter. I was shocked at this and felt like I had to run away from the place. So, I went home and decided to read my mini Gideon's Bible. I read one of the gospels, where they were shouting "Crucify Him!" I felt like I was in the crowd. The next minute, I saw a king sitting on a throne surrounded by jewels, jasper, sapphire, chalcedony, emerald, onyx, sardius, jacinth, amethyst. I did not know that these were in the Bible at the time. (Revelation 21:19) I said to God, "If it's you, do it again." He did. Still needing convincing, I kept on asking "Do it again, do it again, do it again?"

He did. I knew He was real. I asked to see a Christian minister the next day. I told him I wanted to be a Christian and he led me through a prayer of giving my life to Jesus.

My life was never to be the same again.

I spent most of my time sobbing, I was depressed, unemployed and taking one day at a time. My brother got married, my mum and her partner did too. We all became Christians, and all went to the same church. My 10 year old niece was hit by a car on the pavement only the width of a car away from me, it missed me by just a few inches. She flew into the air and landed on her back but an angel protected her. I thought she was dead, so I prayed in tongues and undid her scarf. The neighbour came out and I asked her to call an ambulance. When we went to the hospital, they checked her and all she had was a badly bruised leg. (The driver had lost control of the car because she had an epileptic fit.)

That same night, I heard the Holy Spirit whisper in my ear "Trust in the LORD forever, for the LORD, the LORD himself, is the Rock eternal." (Isaiah 26:4 NIV) I did not know until the next day that the car had gone right into the house; the bricks were demolished under the front window. That was Christmas Eve, in church no-one was able to help me. I remember being there, holding my 2 year old niece, shaking and praying I would not drop her on the concrete floor. I could not stop shaking, I was afraid to cross a road, struggled to breathe, was numb and had asthma for 6 months before the Lord healed me. This, I learnt a number of years later, was the result of trauma. There was also a curse operating in our family; this all happened on the same road where I was hit by a car when I was 10 years old. It was years later when I fully recovered from this trauma, as the Lord taught and healed me from this experience. I got a job in a local supermarket, which I hated. Every day I would pray the scripture that the Lord would sustain me. (Isaiah 46:4)

I loved the scriptures and still do.

I quickly realised my need to be healed from the consequences of bad stuff in my life. I began to forgive, bless and release people who had hurt me. This was a painful process; however God's love and grace was sufficient for me.

I went to a Christian healing centre where I would see the demons who I remembered being in my life as a child. They told me they were never going to leave me. I was terrified, holding on to the lady who was praying for me with my faith holding on by the skin of my teeth. She said to these demons "Don't you hurt her!" and I felt an angel touch my heel. I was filled with strength and thought to myself "How dare they try to hurt me, I'm a child of God!" I shouted at them "Get out of my life, get out of my life. Go on, get out my life!" They were terrified and ran away from us. I then knew that the demons are terrified of the angels and Christians who know their God.

After that weekend away I slept for around 30 minutes a day because the Lord had healed me from fear of sleeping. His peace was tangible.

The following Sunday, I stood up to testify about this, reciting Psalm 9:9 (NIV), which says "The LORD is a refuge for the oppressed, a stronghold in times of trouble. Those who know your name trust in you." I could not stand up. I was asking God why He was doing this to me as I felt embarrassed. The minister explained that it was the Holy Spirit touching me and doing a work in me.

Notes

The Best Church Ever!

I began to thirst for the things of God, I went to revival meetings weekly. I enjoyed experiencing God's love, His joy and the teaching about healing accomplished at the cross.

I had many encounters with the LORD, and they changed me. I began to feel more secure, heard His voice clearly and eventually stopped going to my local church. The Lord told me to move to another town to live, to be part of a new church which He was establishing. I did and was the tenth person to join. It was great, so intimate in fellowship and worship. After a few months, we started to host conferences where hundreds of people came to be refreshed and enjoy God's presence. I was a ministry team leader, prophetic team leader and a life group leader. I loved this, seeing healing and being told my words were accurate.

I fell in love with a man immediately in church. We got married. I knew it was a mistake; I should have heeded God's warning, but it made no sense at the time. After a few weeks of being married, my husband began to insult and reject me. Eating loads of unhealthy take-aways, I put on 50 kgs of weight in a few years. I was very ill and had a stomach valve and a hernia fixed. This was no life for me. Over time, drinking alcohol to cope with his drunkenness and mine led to us being stopped from having a weekly life group in our home. I was glad of this. However, our pastors were unable to support us as much as we needed to be. They tried, but we could not stop drinking.

We went to another church where we were welcomed initially. It was not a good experience for us. We were accused of gossiping, which was a lie to cover those who were. Because we were so unhappy both at church and home, we were both drinking much more than what was good for us, though of course we could not see that. I had a full-time job working with disaffected young people in alternative provision for children excluded from mainstream education. Most of them were abused, neglected in some way, coming from dysfunctional families with histories of crime, domestic violence and drug and alcohol abuse.

It was only through God's grace and strength that I was able to do the job with some empathy. After 8 years working there, I was made redundant, so I decided to go on a three-week training school about healing. I was deeply impacted by this. The Lord healed me from the trauma of being hit by a car when I was 10 years old. He also reminded me that He called me from before I was born and was going to repay me for the years that the locusts had eaten.

Whilst I felt I had received a level of healing, I was not encouraged to believe or walk it out; as a result things at home got worse than ever before. Our relationship deteriorated to the extent that I ended up in a women's refuge.

Traumatised and lost, I still went to church by train. I lost my friends who thought I should just sort stuff out with my husband. I could not sense the Lord's presence or hear Him. No-one in my family came to visit me. Lost, alone, lights on, no-one home.

The second refuge I was in was nearer my family. Then I got a flat where I still live. I went to a local church where I found that people still expected you to reconcile with your spouse because God would give you strength to cope.

Another church, same advice. Still numb, confused dot com.

Thank the Lord, I met an old friend who invited me to her home church. This is now my home where I have received the most love, acceptance, healing and deliverance ever.

Healing is not just a one-off experience, it's a continuous process, being changed into the image of Jesus. There have been so many changes in my life so far, I am amazed at His love, His commitment to us all. I want to encourage you to seek the Lord for this. It is your inheritance. He wants to give you ALL that is rightfully yours! He knows you TOTALLY.

He knows you through and through and through. You did not choose Him, but He chose you!

A Poem

Don't You Know?

Don't you know?
You are unique
The real you is all I seek
Your life is and always has been in My hands
You're totally accepted and included in My plans.

I am always here, I will never leave you
I know you through and through and through
Yes, the real you!

Yes, I see your flaws
Your shortcomings, bad attitude, indifference, when
you're angry or rude
Still and forever My love is totally yours.

Don't you know?

You came from Me
Not of natural descent or a father's will, but born of God.

Don't you know everything I have is yours?
Yes, all of it! Everything!

Don't you know?
I can see, I am longing to set you free
From all the pain, shame, rejection, neglect, loneliness,
isolation, the lot!

Will you trust Me with your life so fragile?
My touch is gentle not harsh
Not what you have been accustomed to...
Different in every way and form.

Not domineering, self-centred, cruel, harsh or blind
You have been and are always on My mind
Yes, I understand it will take you time. One step at a time
Will you come and rest with Me a while?

This was written as I was, and still am, recovering from the trauma and effects of domestic violence. A lot of sobbing was done.

Notes

An Invitation for Today

He is inviting you to be with Him today. To just be, if you want to.

You may need to go somewhere quiet to be alone: He is waiting. He will meet you with a warm, pure, loving smile. Don't let anything stop you, because something will try to.

"Choose life!"

If this means telling God how you feel in words no-one else will understand or telling Him how disappointed or indifferent you are at this moment then tell Him, He loves to hear you. He will heal you!

Only He knows everything about you. He wants to share His life with you. He will reveal His secrets to you.

"The secret [of the sweet, satisfying companionship] of the LORD have they who fear (revere and worship) Him, He will show them His covenant and reveal to them its [deep inner] meaning" (Psalm 25:14)

You can have authentic, different, close and meaningful times in your relationship with Him.

The best, most secure loving relationships are authentic. In and through your authentic, sincere relationship with Him you will discover more!

Automatically, you will be able to recover more! These go hand in hand!

It's a wonderful, eternal cycle. I love being in it! How wonderful it is to have fellowship with our perfect Father!

"Be perfect, therefore, as your heavenly Father is perfect." (Matthew 5:48 NIV)

If you had bad experiences with your father, it will continue to be a process to know this is the truth; God understands this and will do absolutely EVERYTHING to convince you who He really is.

I struggled and felt bad as I wanted to trust the Lord with my life. One day He said to me out of the blue "Do you think I don't understand or appreciate the fact that you don't trust Me as much as you think you should? Do you think I don't understand?"

Of course, He does. Please know this; He will take you one step at a time. Your life with Him will not be exactly the same as anyone else's. It will be intimate, which means private and personal. You don't have to share it with anyone if you don't want to, you are not obligated to so either.

Some secrets are not to be shared.

One day I felt a bit down, and again unexpectedly the Lord said, "I want you to be successful Antoinette." I wondered what success meant, then before I could think about it, He said "And success is wholeness, you're not there yet but you're getting there!"

Is your life in a mess? Do you want success? Then say "Yes" to the process!

Before I continue, I think it is important to let you know that there will be times when you do not come to Him... This is also part of the process of discovering and recovering.

A Poem

My Love Is Greater Than It All

My love is deeper than it all!
I am here constantly, I understand why you don't come to Me
I am taking those things away
Shame, guilt, confusion, your brokenness, ALL of it.

I am jealous for your affection
You are always in My reach, I am here, I am here.

I was when you were all alone in your bed
I've heard everything said and unsaid.

Yes, every word, whisper and groan
I made you, you're Mine... ALWAYS and FOREVER.

How could I reject you?
You are My treasured possession, bought at a price by the precious blood of My Son Jesus
All the broken promises and lies
Were not from Me but from an angel of light in disguise.

This was written while recovering from losing friends in church, my home and possessions.

Discovering and recovering is a process, where we co-operate with the Lord through a relationship with Him.

Notes

Definition of Process

Definition of Process:

A series of actions or steps taken in order to achieve a particular end. A series of events performed to make something or achieve a particular result or a series of changes that happen naturally.

To deal with something according to a set of actions.

To process information is to take in, absorb, understand, remember and put into order and apply it to your life.

"That people may know skilful and godly wisdom and instruction, discern and comprehend the words of understanding and insight. Receive instruction in wise dealing and the disciplines of wise thoughtfulness, righteousness, justice and integrity. That prudence may be given to the simple and knowledge, discretion and discernment to the youth. The wise will hear then increase in learning and the person of understanding will acquire skill and attain sound counsel so that he may be able to steer his course rightly." (Proverbs 1:1-5)

"Give instruction to wise man and he will yet be wiser, teach a righteous man (one upright and in right standing with God) and he will increase in learning." (Proverbs 9:9)

We all need to learn, to gain more understanding so we can progress into our God given destinies. How we learn is different; so God will teach you in a very distinctive, very personal way. It is part of the process, it is necessary and gives us more of a hope for the future.

He made your brain, its processing abilities, memory, recall and imagination.

A Poem

Every Cell

Every brain cell, cortex, nerve and synapse
Used to full potential, My plan for you will not change or collapse
So vast
At last.
Come aside, don't hide, I can see
Yes, it is coming into view
I will not disappoint you, your deferred hope is coming to an end!

A short poem written at work recently.

It is your Father's desire, His good pleasure to give you the kingdom.

"Do not be afraid little flock because your Father is pleased to give you the kingdom." (Luke 12:32 NIV)

"If you then, though you are evil know how to give good gifts to your children, then how much more will your Father in heaven give good gifts to those who ask Him?" (Matthew 7:11 NIV)

What are you asking Him for? Maybe you're not even sure what it is yet.

Just speak to Him, tell Him whatever you want to. He already knows what you are going to say.

Notes

The Need for More Recovery

My older brother was an alcoholic; drinking from a young age he would eventually become homeless, living in and out of hostels. He had no interest in sport, women, television or anything else in life. I remember him being filthy dirty, with grimy hands and face, only able to say "Sound, sound as pound." He would stagger down the street. He, my sister and I would drink pints of sherry bought from the local shop, alongside the home-made beer which tasted horrible; we did not care though. We drank it out of mugs. On one occasion, our three-year-old niece drank some and we did not notice. We realised when she became floppy, and we were very scared. Fortunately, her nan came in, she went ballistic at us for being so irresponsible. Taken to A and E, my niece was left to sleep it off. There were no medical problems. My sister got grounded, our mum never heard about it.

Our younger brother also started to drink heavily too. He had a great job but had to leave because of frequent absences. My sister settled down and had her first child at 17 years old. We became close and still are. She had another two children and is now a proud grandma to six grandchildren. Our dad went to live with our older brother because his wife threw him out due to accusations made against him. Their windows were smashed in and their three-year-old granddaughter, my older sister's first child, was very traumatised by this. She was not taken into care, but her other eight siblings born after her were all fostered by the same family. My older sister suffered from manic depression, and she was beaten by her husband. They just could not cope with having children. I remember her becoming hysterical at one point because she thought her daughter was lost. She was sectioned a few times, staying in a psychiatric hospital until she recovered. She had a great sense of humour, I guess this is how she coped. She died from spine cancer aged 51 years, living in a care home for a few months before she died. She was the life and soul of the party. I held her hand with her daughter and my husband as she passed away. I told her if she wanted to go to heaven with Jesus she could, because He died for her. She walked straight into heaven. It was so bright and beautiful, pure love and light filled the room. I wanted to follow her. She was at peace at long last.

Six months before her premature death, my older brother was murdered by his drunken friends who literally kicked his head in in broad daylight. Passers-by were shocked and called the police. It was all recorded on the CCTV cameras. I was so very, very angry, as would be expected. No-one in church could help, their prayers were futile I thought. Some could not give me any eye contact. His body was frozen for six months for forensic examination to be carried out as evidence for the prosecution in court. It was sickening to think about.

Notes

He Knows You

God made us look like we do. All our physical features, body parts, our size, shape, eye, hair and skin colour. He also created our inmost beings. (Psalm 139:13)

"The very hairs of your head are all numbered." (Luke 12:7 NIV)

Our sense of humour, thought processes, imagination, our use of language, words, even all our intelligences. Our personal likes and dislikes of food, music, interests, hobbies, subjects, good and bad habits and general outlook on life... He knows all our hopes and fears, our reservations, negative and positive attitudes towards people, things that we are not at all interested in and all the things that make us tick and feel alive. We could read through lists of adjectives describing ourselves; God knows us all PERFECTLY and intimately.

He cares for us. "Cast all your anxiety on Him because He cares for you." (1 Peter 5:7 NIV)

He wants to talk to us about these things. He has got so much more to say to us!

In areas where we reject ourselves, He wants to heal us so we can accept ourselves as He made us. Our TRUE selves. The need for love precedes the discovery of our talents and abilities. We often do not let others see the TRUE "me" because we are afraid of being rejected. We please others instead of being ourselves, we take on a false identity.

God wants us to be ourselves, to live in our TRUE identity. God made you as you are and wants you to fulfil His purpose for your life.

"The Lord will perfect that which concerns me. Your mercy and loving kindness O Lord, endure forever - forsake not the works of your own hands." (Psalm 138:8)

He will not change His mind about His purposes for your life.

"For God's gifts and his call are irrevocable." (Romans 11:29 NIV)

To perfectly fulfil His purposes for our lives we must be ourselves, which means that some false identity will have to be removed from us.

"For I know the plans I have for you," declares the LORD, "plans to prosper you and not to harm you, plans to give you hope and a future." (Jeremiah 29:11 NIV)

How well you discover and recover is dependent on your willingness to co-operate with the Lord during the process.

"Choose life!"

"The thief comes only to steal, kill and destroy; I have come that you might have life and have it to the FULL!" (John 10:10 NIV)

Notes

Hearing His Voice

Discovering: Hearing God, that is how we find out what He wants to reveal to us. We will be asking Him questions throughout, so we know what He is saying to us personally. We will be journaling, which is a simple exercise of listening, hearing and writing down what He is saying.

Jesus says, "My sheep listen to My voice; I know them, and they follow Me" (John 10:27 NIV)

We can be confident this is true!...

How to journal... from "Communion with God" by Dr Mark Virkler[1].

Firstly, position yourself, look to see what God will say.

"I will stand at my watch and station myself on the ramparts; I will look and see what He will say to me." (Habakkuk 2:1 NIV)

Remove distractions, thoughts of things demanding your attention, leave them aside, they can wait. This is a time set aside to be with and commune with God.

---

[1] Mark Virkler, *Communion with God* (Shippensburg, Pennsylvania: Destiny Image Publishers, 2001)

Be still, relax, be comfortable, rest.

"Be still and know that I am God." (Psalm 46:10 NIV)

"Do not fret or have any anxiety about anything, but in every circumstance and in everything by prayer and petition [definite requests], with thanksgiving, continue to make your wants known to God." (Philippians 4:6)

Still your soul.

"But I have calmed and quieted myself." (Psalm 131:2 NIV)

Tune into spontaneous thoughts, pictures and words. Recognise this is how God speaks. Write down the revelation, what you see and hear. Write it on paper.

"Write down the revelation and make it plain on tablets." (Habakkuk 2:2 NIV)

Ask God this question...

What do you think of me at this very moment?

Write down what He says to you.

God has a timescale.

God determined the times set in all of history.

"But when the set time had fully come, God sent His Son." (Galatians 4:4 NIV)

"When the times reach their fulfilment." (Ephesians 1:10 NIV)

"For we are God's [own] handiwork [His workmanship] recreated in Christ Jesus, [born anew] that we may do those good works which God predestined [planned beforehand] for us [taking paths which He prepared ahead of time], that we should walk in them [living the good life which He prearranged and made ready for us to live.]" (Ephesians 2:10)

"Your eyes saw my unformed substance, and in your book all the days [of my life] were written before ever they took shape, when as yet there was none of them." (Psalm 139:16)

"My times are in Your hands." (Psalm 31:15 NIV)

"He made from one [common origin, one source, one blood] all nations of men to settle on the face of the earth, having definitely determined [their] allotted periods of time." (Acts 17:26)

Talk to Him about a specific time in your life, ask questions if you want to.

Notes

The Subject of Shame

Shame first came into the world when man sinned. "The eyes of both of them were opened and they realised they were naked; so they sewed fig leaves and made coverings for themselves." (Genesis 3:7 NIV)

Shame, in its essence, makes us want to cover up, making us afraid and want to hide from God and other people.

We all have some shame in our lives. It makes us feel bad and think "I am a mistake, I'm flawed, I'm bad, I'm ashamed." We think "What if they find out? Will they reject me?" or "I will control everything so that they won't find out what I am really like, so I will not get hurt or suffer pain."

We hide ourselves, just like Adam and Eve did. We can also believe a lie that God made a mistake making us. This is a MASSIVE lie! Satan is a liar and keeps lying to us. It is imperative for us to know the truth, that is what will set us free!

"He was a murderer from the beginning, not holding to the truth, for there is NO truth in him. When he lies, he speaks his native language, for he is a LIAR and the father of lies." (John 8:44 NIV)

"So Jesus said to those Jews who had believed in Him "If you abide in My word [hold fast to My teachings and live in accordance with them], you are truly My disciples. And you will know the Truth and the Truth will set you free" (John 8:31-32)

God never makes mistakes. He is PERFECT!

"Be perfect, therefore, as your heavenly Father is perfect." (Matthew 5:48 NIV)

He understands that we see Him as we have seen our natural dads who are imperfect and that we judge Him the same way; He will show Himself to us!

"All things have been committed to Me by My Father. No one knows the Son except the Father and no one knows the Father except the Son and those whom the Son chooses to reveal Him." (Matthew 11:27 NIV)

You have been chosen to know your PERFECT heavenly Father!

This is the start of a wonderful process of knowing Him, where we choose to believe what He says about us instead of believing lies about Him and where we accept Him as He really is.

We all need our minds renewing.

"Do not conform to the pattern of this world but be transformed by the renewing of your mind. Then you will be able to test and approve what God's will is - His good, pleasing and perfect will." (Romans 12:2 NIV)

He has got a totally perfect, pleasing and good destiny for each one of us!

Let us continue discovering who He is, who we are and His purposes for our lives. He even knows what you are thinking this very moment!

Ask Him questions....

Who am I?

Where am I on your timescale?

Notes

Your Unique Intelligences

Which are your strong intelligences?

Put a circle around the numbers of these descriptions that you feel apply to you.

1. You can remember quotes or nice turns of phrase and can use them in conversation.

2. You sense quickly when someone you are with is troubled or bothered about something.

3. You are fascinated by scientific and philosophical questions like "When did time begin?"

4. You can find your way around a new area or neighbourhood very quickly.

5. You are good at using your hands and you rarely feel awkward in your movements.

6. You can sing in tune.

7. You regularly look at television programmes or magazines on science, technology or computing or read the science pages in a newspaper.

8. You note other people's errors in words or grammar even if you don't correct them.

9.   You can often work out how something works or how to fix something that is broken without asking for help.

10.   You can imagine how other people play the roles they do in their work or families and you can put yourself in their shoes.

11.   You can remember in detail the layout and landmarks of places you have visited when on holiday.

12.   You enjoy music and have favourite performers.

13.   You like to draw or paint.

14.   You dance well.

15.   You organise and arrange things in your kitchen, bathroom, bedroom or desk according to categories and in patterns.

16.   You feel confident in interpreting why other people behave as they do.

17.   You like to tell stories and are considered to be a good storyteller.

18.   You sometimes enjoy different sounds in your environment, or you play a musical instrument.

19.   When you meet new people, you often make connections between their characteristics and those of other people you know.

20.   You feel you have a keen sense of what you can do and what you don't want to do.

Now look at the following triplets of numbers. If you possess two out of any triplet, underline it once. If you have circled three numbers in any triplet, then double underline it. You are probably very strong in that intelligence even if you have not developed it.

Descriptions 1, 8 and 17. (Linguistic)

Descriptions 3, 7 and 15. (Logical / Mathematical)

Descriptions 4, 11 and 13. (Visual / Spatial)

Descriptions 6, 12 and 18. (Musical)

Descriptions 5, 9 and 14. (Kinaesthetic)

Descriptions 2, 10 and 19. (Interpersonal)

Descriptions 10, 16 and 20. (Intrapersonal)

Whatever your strong intelligences might be, you can find ways to use them; either by using them in the way you learn, or in using them to help you to choose what you might enjoy doing as a vocation (what you do as a vocation can often be your "calling", something God specifically has for you to do here on earth.)

Our main educational systems mainly teach and train just two intelligences which are:

Linguistic Intelligence- skill with words as exemplified by writers and negotiators.

Logical / Mathematical Intelligence - skill in analysis and logic as exemplified by economists, scientists, and computer programmers.

There is no question that these are important intelligences but there are five others:

Visual / Spatial - the ability to visualise and create images in your mind's eye as exemplified by architects, navigators, artists, photographers, designers, florists, and chefs.

Musical - the ability to create and identify complex patterns of sound as exemplified by musicians, sound mixers, disc jockeys, and speech therapists.

Kinaesthetic - the ability to use physical intelligence as exemplified by surgeons, plumbers, mechanics, engineers, and joiners.

People who are good with their hands don't often recognise that they are demonstrating a higher intelligence.

Interpersonal - the ability to communicate well, to be empathetic as exemplified by personal trainers, parents, customer service personnel, counsellors, and nursery nurses.

Intrapersonal - the ability to create one's own goals and plans, to be reflective of one's own behaviour as a guide to future action.

High I.Q. is not an accurate indicator of success, there are lots of people who have this and are miserable and unsuccessful.

"I praise you because I am fearfully and wonderfully made; your works are wonderful!" (Psalm 139:14)

There never has been, or ever will be, anyone exactly like you!

Rejoice in your uniqueness!

Notes

A Terrible Trauma

It was the worst time ever when my eldest brother was murdered. The court hearing was horrendous. The video of the attack was played 10 times. I did not watch it but left the court. I was furious seeing the accused; their defences and excuses were ridiculous. They both served 13 years each. I was traumatised, shocked and angry alongside my siblings. I knew I needed to forgive them; this took time until eventually I was able to release them. Bitterness and resentment would not steal my faith.

The police came and asked me if I wanted to see my brother's body before he was cremated as it had to be quick because of how he was decaying. I agreed. I went into a small room and saw him lying there; behind him I saw two spirits, the one behind him was Murder, the one behind that one was Death. They said to me, "Look at what we can do, look at our power!" I was so shocked at this I started to scream, I went hysterical and ran out of the building. My other brother was also in a state of shock. The police were there for us and called my husband to take us home, which he did. I was so traumatised by this event I had to have time off from work. No-one in church knew what to do with me. I was so numb, just going through the motions of being in church, not knowing God's presence like I usually did. Then, one evening, after a church meeting, a visiting speaker who spoke with my husband and who knew what had happened to me asked if she could pray for me. I said "Yes." She told all the spirits of death, murder and all sorts to leave me. They screamed and screamed. I was free from their influence. The following day, a lady asked me what was going on with my screaming the night before. She said it sounded like I was being murdered. I told her that my brother was. I hate these demons, but I know Jesus is much greater. He has a great vengeance for them all! Alleluia!!!!!

I knew the Bible to be true when I heard in my spirit and read these verses...

"The last enemy to be subdued and abolished is death!" (1 Corinthians 15:26)

"Where, O death is your victory? Where, O death is your sting?" (1 Corinthians 15:55 NIV)

When my sister died aged 51, it was only three days before my brother's funeral, and it was also on my husband's birthday. This was a very tough, harsh time for our family. These deaths were shocking to say the least, all we could do was to support, help, and be there for each other.

This was such a dark time in my life, I often wonder how I got through it. As I look back, I can see how the Lord carried and sustained me throughout that time, even when I was unaware of it.

Notes

Personal Promises

What are the personal promises God has given to you so far?

Write them down, then ask Him to give you another one. Listen, hear His voice, then write down what He says to you.

This will encourage you, build, cheer and lift you up!

It is HOPE for your future, which is already planned and before you. Don't worry if you cannot see it yet, it will come into view over time.

You will be able to join the dots as you continue to discover and recover!

Talk to Him about your 'Unique Intelligences'…. listen to Him too, write down what He says to you!

Notes

God's Intentions for Our Lives

His main intention is to make us like His Son.

"And we all, who with unveiled faces contemplate the LORD's glory, are being transformed with ever increasing glory, which comes from the LORD, who is the Spirit." (2 Corinthians 3:18 NIV)

"In your relationships with each other, have the same mindset as Christ Jesus: Who, in being very nature God, did not consider equality with God something to be used to His own advantage; rather, He made Himself nothing by taking on the nature of a servant, being made in human likeness. And being found in the appearance of a man, He humbled Himself by becoming obedient to death – even death on a cross!" (Philippians 2:5-8 NIV)

"But just as He who called you is holy, so be holy in all you do; for it is written: 'Be holy, because I am holy.'" (1 Peter 1:15-16 NIV)

The things that God says to us will always make us more like Jesus. In fact, He wants us to have the best life we could possibly have, which is found only in Him.

Fullness of Life

"If the world hates you, keep in mind it hated me first. If you belonged to the world, it would love you as its own. As it is, you do not belong to this world, but I have chosen you out of the world. (John 15:18-19 NIV)

"But our citizenship is in heaven." (Philippians 3:20 NIV)

"The Spirit of Truth. The world cannot accept Him, because it neither sees Him or knows Him. But you know Him, for He lives with you and will be in you." (John 14:17 NIV)

We are now children of God, we are in the world but not of it. The world's pleasures will never truly satisfy us, only God's love in Christ and everything in His kingdom, which is ours, will do.

"Truly my soul finds rest in God; my salvation comes from Him." (Psalm 62:1 NIV)

As we get to know Him more, we will find this is true.

Notes

Jehovah Rapha
The God Who Heals

"I am the LORD, who heals you." (Exodus 15:26)

It is God's very nature to heal, and, because of the fall of man, we all need some healing to some extent in our lives.

"For all have sinned and fall short of the glory of God, and all are justified freely by His grace through the redemption that came by Jesus Christ." (Romans 3:23-24 NIV)

"Therefore if any person is [ingrafted] in Christ [The Messiah] he is a new creation [a new creature altogether]; the old, [previous moral and spiritual condition] has passed away. Behold, the fresh and new has come!" (2 Corinthians 5:17)

Redemption, forgiveness of sins, being a new creation, having eternal life, which is knowing God as He really is, are the beginning of wholeness. This is spiritual healing, being able to come home to where we really belong with our Father in heaven, sharing life with Jesus and the Holy Spirit. Here we can access ALL the healing we will ever need in any and every area of our lives!

"Praise the LORD, my soul and forget not His benefits-who forgives ALL your sins and heals ALL your diseases, who redeems your life from the pit and crowns you with love and compassion, who satisfies your desires with good things so that your youth is renewed like the eagle's." (Psalm 103:2-5 NIV)

Healing of the Spirit

Jesus came to heal broken-hearted people; He fulfilled the prophecy that Isaiah said He would do.

"He has sent me to bind up the brokenhearted, to proclaim freedom for the captives and release from darkness for the prisoners." (Isaiah 61:1 NIV)

"Anxiety in a man's heart weighs it down, but an encouraging word makes it glad." (Proverbs 12:25)

"The LORD is near to the broken hearted and saves those who are crushed in spirit." (Psalm 34:18 NIV)

"A cheerful heart is good medicine, but a crushed spirit dries up the bones." (Proverbs 17:22 NIV)

"The human spirit can endure in sickness, but a crushed spirit, who can bear?" (Proverbs 18:14 NIV)

"A happy heart makes the face cheerful but heartache crushes the spirit." (Proverbs 15:13 NIV)

Is there an area in your life where you feel your spirit is crushed?

Talk to Him about it, then a close friend if you need to.

Jesus will heal this by pouring out His love, compassion and comfort into your spirit. He will minister to you personally and appropriately because He knows you inside out.

He is humble and gentle in spirit.

Healing of the Mind

Our thoughts direct our behaviour, actions, choices, and the decisions we make.

"For as he thinks in his heart, so is he. As one who reckons, he says to you, eat and drink, yet his heart is not with you [but is grudging the cost]." (Proverbs 23:7)

This is why we need to let our thoughts be subjected to the Lord and let our minds constantly be renewed.

"We take every thought captive and make it obedient to Christ." (2 Corinthians 10 :5)

"Be transformed by the renewing of your mind." (Romans 12:2 NIV)

"Those who live according to the flesh have their minds set on what the flesh desires; but those who live according to the Spirit have their minds set on what the Spirit desires. The mind governed by the flesh is death, but the mind governed by the Spirit is life and peace. The mind governed by the flesh is hostile to God; it does not submit to God's law; nor can it do so. Those who are in the realm of the flesh cannot please God." (Romans 8:5-8 NIV)

We all want to live in the Spirit; to do this we must choose to do so, meaning we let Him govern our thinking which leads to life. Our enemy will also put negative thoughts into our minds, we must recognise this so we can choose to ignore and reject them, submitting to God's thoughts, which are always good and full of life. So it is a REAL struggle and battle for our minds. Are there any thoughts that constantly bombard your mind? Where do they come from? Your flesh (self), enemy or God? What actions do they lead you to do?

Choose life!

Speak to and ask God. Talk to a trusted friend if you need to as well.

Write down what He says and be obedient.

Healing of the Body

Jesus went around doing good and healing everyone who needed healing.

"Jesus Christ is the same yesterday, today and forever." (Hebrews 13:8 NIV)

Whatever He did on earth, He still does today. Think of the physical healings He did, how differently He did each one, meeting the unique needs of each person. In John's gospel chapter 5, there was a man who was waiting to get into a pool to get healed. He believed in its healing virtues. He was an invalid for 38 years and was surrounded by others like himself. Jesus asked him if he wanted to get well; lacking confidence and not expecting Jesus to heal him, he said that while he tries to get in the water, someone else goes in ahead of him. "Get up! Pick up your mat and walk." said Jesus. At once the man was cured, picked up his mat and walked. Sometimes, we do not expect to be healed; being surrounded by others like ourselves we have relied on other things to make us whole, just like this man did before Jesus healed him. We also need to hear Jesus and do what He says, the man's simple faith in responding to Jesus' instructions allowed this miracle to happen. (John 5:1-8)

At other times we need to push past the crowd, like the woman with the issue of blood who had spent all her money on doctors and was still not cured. She thought that if only she could touch His cloak she would be healed. Using the great faith she had, she touched Him. Jesus knew someone did because power had come out of Him, causing her to confess it was her. His response was beautiful, "Daughter, your faith has healed you. Go in peace." (Luke 8:43-48 NIV)

A centurion said to Jesus, "Lord, my servant lies at home paralysed, suffering terribly." Jesus asked him "Shall I come and heal him?" The centurion told Him to just say the word and his servant would be healed. Jesus was amazed at his faith, then said to him "Go! Let it be done just as you believed it would!" And his servant was healed that very moment. (Matthew 8:5-14 NIV)

Jesus ALWAYS responds to faith, whatever size it is!

"A man with Leprosy came and knelt before Him and said "Lord, if you are willing you can make me clean." "I am willing." He said, "Be clean!" Immediately he was cleansed from his Leprosy." (Matthew 8:2-4 NIV)

Once, Jesus healed a man born blind: "After saying this, he spat on the ground, made some mud with the saliva, and put it on the man's eyes. "Go," he told him, "wash in the Pool of Siloam (this word means "Sent"). So the man went and washed, and came home seeing." (John 9:6-7 NIV)

There are other healings He did. Do you need any physical healing? What are you expecting, are you waiting, asking someone to ask for you or going straight ahead to touch Jesus?

What will you discover, then recover?

Again, this is a very personal response to God. Can you talk and listen to Him? Is there anyone who you would like to ask Jesus to heal?

Jesus even raised the dead; He still does!

One day, His heart went out to a widow whose son had died. He said, "Don't cry." He touched the coffin which he was being carried in, He said "Young man, I say to you, get up!" The dead man sat up and began to talk then Jesus gave him back to his mother. (Luke 7:13-15 NIV)

Another day, Jesus' heart went out to his friends, Mary and Martha; their brother Lazarus had died. Jesus was deeply moved and when He saw where they had buried him told them to "Take away the stone." He prayed to His Father, thanking Him that He heard Him always; but this was for the benefit of the people standing there that they might believe that His Father sent Him. He then called in a loud voice "Lazarus, come out!" The dead man came out, his hands and feet wrapped in strips of linen and a cloth around his face. Jesus said to them "Take off the grave clothes and let him go." (John 11:38-44 NIV)

Jesus only has to speak, and healings and resurrections happen!

Emotional Healing

Our emotions are important to the Lord. They can be hurt, ignored, crushed, or battered causing damage which causes us pain. We often do not take our feelings seriously, maybe thinking that we have to overcome and gain victory over them, as if they don't exist. We can tend to push them down, especially if we don't understand why they are surfacing. They usually do surface, because the Lord wants to heal them. Any harsh words or sarcasm, being rejected, misunderstood, treated badly, betrayed, shamed, lied against, gossiped about or any type of abusive behaviour towards us causes emotional pain. It is often done unknowingly and unintentionally. Emotional pain needs to be given to God, otherwise we will carry unnecessary pain and burdens, which have the potential to make us physically sick too. This is called psychosomatic Illness. The Lord will bring to your memory the things that caused the pain; it can be triggered by certain tunes, places, sounds, smells, tastes or sights because it is all stored in the memory. The Holy Spirit will comfort you, as you release the pain you will be able to forgive those who hurt you and caused the pain. Forgiveness is necessary. Sometimes it takes time but the Lord will help you as you choose to do it. He really wants to free you from these painful emotions.

"Praise be to the God and Father of our Lord Jesus Christ, the Father of compassion and the God of all comfort, who comforts us in all our troubles so that we can comfort those in any trouble with the comfort we ourselves receive from God." (2 Corinthians 1:3-4 NIV)

"For the LORD comforts His people and will have compassion on His afflicted ones." (Isaiah 49:13 NIV)

As a mother comforts her child, so I will comfort you." (Isaiah 66:13 NIV)

"Your rod and staff, they comfort me." (Psalm 23:4 NIV)

"I will ask the Father and He will give you another Comforter (Counsellor, Intercessor, Advocate, Strengthener, and Standby) that He may remain with you forever." (John 14:15-16)

You will find many more scriptures about God's comfort.

The Holy Spirit will also remind you of the things Jesus has said to you.

"But the Advocate, The Holy Spirit, whom the Father will send in My Name will teach you all things and will remind you of everything I have said to you." (John 14:26 NIV)

Is there anything you would like to ask Jesus about?

Certain memories, their effects on you?

Your responses to certain stimuli?

Other questions? Talk to Him, He is listening at this very moment.

A Poem

Lotions, Potions, Ideas and Notions

Lotions, potions, ideas and notions
He's got all the perfect remedies and answers
for ALL your personal questions
His love is deeper than all the oceans.

Will they do the trick when you're sick?
Ask Him if you dare
Healing balm for a broken arm, for your anxiety, calm
A pure love to shatter and dispel your shame.

It is true, He knows your name
Like your neighbour, you are uniquely made, not exactly
the same
Yes, He knows your frame.

Do you feel shattered, battered, your life scattered?
Lost in a zone, when you're all alone?
Afraid to look under that stone?
He is your comfort, strength and power.
You ARE His
Never alone and surrounded by heavenly hosts.

He is the Great I AM, no-one else comes close!

Try not to despise, look up to the skies, open your eyes
Choose to ignore and reject the lies
Because He hears ALL of your cries.

This was written when I was thinking of how, however the world tries, it cannot truly give perfect healing in every aspect of an individual's life like God can and does.

I encourage you to be transparent with God as much as you are able to because...

He is with you!

He has your best interests in His heart and it goes out to you!

His compassion for you is real and vast!

He will be and is everything you will ever need!

He will carry, sustain, and rescue you!

You will be truly fulfilled as you get to know Him more!

He knows YOUR name!

He has written a book about you, your life!

Nothing has or ever can separate you from His love, ever!

Notes

The Effects of Transgression and Iniquity

"He was pierced for our **transgressions**, He was crushed for our **iniquities**." (Isaiah 53:5 NIV)

He was punished for these things in our lives, we can now have peace with God. These two words are not often used in everyday language or heard in churches much. However, it is vital to understand what transgression is and what iniquity is; their origin, patterns, cycles in relationships, the way they determine behaviour and the consequences of it. They are inherited and are influenced by our human nature, which in the Bible is referred to as the sinful nature.

Definition of Transgress: To break a rule or law. Break, contravene, defy, disobey, flout, infringe, violate.

Transgression: Error, fault, misdeed, misdemeanour, offence, wrongdoing, violation.

Definition of Iniquity: Wickedness, evil.

Iniquity means "twisted and distorted." It is, in fact, anything that turns away from God's straight and perfect path. It is a spiritual inheritance, impregnated in us at the moment of conception, causing our hearts to be filled with thoughts and intentions opposed to God's righteousness, truth and love; or, in other words, it is the total of all that is evil in mankind. It operates as a 'spiritual umbilical cord' that transmits the spiritual DNA of evil from one generation to the rest, so we are all born with iniquity and we transgress.[2]

However, we can be free from this effect on our lives because Jesus took our punishment and we can have peace with God and ourselves.

For further information on the subject of Iniquity, I recommend Ana Mendez-Ferrell's book called 'Iniquity.'[3]

Our character traits will be the same or very similar to our parents, just like our physical ones, we will commit the same sins and have the same patterns of behaviour. We will have the same or very similar weaknesses, be tempted by the same temptations and unable to resist some of them, having strong desires which cannot be overcome. We may become addicted to certain substances, lifestyles and have tendencies to commit certain acts. Children with parents who are alcoholics or substance addicts will have a strong tendency to behave in the same way. Those with violent tendencies, promiscuity, any sexual aberrations, adulterous or divorced parents will pass these patterns of behaviour to

---

[2] Ana Mendez-Ferrel, *Iniquity, (*Voice Of The Light Ministries, Incorporated, 2017)
[3] Ibid.

their children. Other iniquitous patterns of behaviour are stubbornness, fraudulent activities, financial problems, debt, fear, stress, unbelief, rejection, lust and affliction or any religious activity that becomes false worship, meaning it is given more importance than Jesus Himself.

"Wash me thoroughly [and repeatedly] from my iniquity *and* guilt and cleanse me *and* make me wholly pure from my sin!."

"Behold, I was brought forth in [a state of] iniquity; my mother was sinful who conceived me [and I too am sinful]."

"Hide your face from my sins and blot out all my guilt *and* iniquities."

(Psalm 51:2;5;9)

I encourage you to find more scriptures about transgression and iniquity. They are throughout the Bible.

David knew these forces at work in his life. His awareness of this caused him to confess his struggles with them to God.

I thank God that recently He has pulled up the roots of alcoholism, fear, religion, depression and hopelessness out of my life. I no longer have the temptation to drink alcohol, it never crosses my mind. My worship of Jesus is no longer reliant on church services, worship music or any other past experiences of Him. I am extremely hopeful for the future and free from the fear of demonic forces around me.

Iniquity was present in my life from when I was born, in my spiritual DNA. I had to acknowledge these things; some were only revealed to me by the Holy Spirit, then I had to repent of my iniquities and those in my family, back thousands and thousands of years. Iniquity first came into the world when man sinned, it was found in the archangel spoken of in the Bible, who is recognised as Satan.

"You were perfect in your ways from the day you were created, till iniquity was found in you.... You defiled the sanctuaries by the multitude of your iniquities, by the iniquity of your trading." (Ezekiel 28:15, 18 NIV)

Another scripture to add, which shows that iniquity passes down all the generations is this:

"For I, the LORD your God, *am* a jealous God, visiting the iniquity of the fathers upon the children to the third and fourth *generations* of those who hate Me, but showing mercy to thousands, to those who love Me and keep My commandments." (Exodus 20: 5-6 NKJV)

You do not have to live with the consequences of your ancestors' and your own iniquities because of what Jesus has done at the cross, once and for all, for every generation in the whole of history.

I encourage you to talk to someone you can trust and be transparent with them and Jesus. He already knows about your whole life, even before you were born, how iniquity and Satan would try to destroy your life. It does not have to be so. Jesus has made every provision for you to be free from the consequences of ALL transgression and iniquity!

Choose life!

Again, I emphasise that this healing is and will be a process. Jesus will take you at your own pace, trust Him as much as you can.

A Poem

There's a Side of Yourself

There's a side of yourself you want to hide
I understand, I can see why you don't trust Me as much
as you think you should.

Come near, take a tiny step
Do not be afraid
Because the price of your freedom has been paid.

I know you have strayed
Gone your own way, got lost and dismayed
Been betrayed.

I am waiting
You will only find love, forgiveness and grace
You have not or won't ever lose your place.

Let love change you forever.

I am in you, don't you know?
I understand your ways, thoughts and plans
Your tender heart is like clay in My hands.

And I am delighted.

Will you let Me mould you?

My plans will give you a hope and a future
Plans to prosper you and not to harm you.

Is this all new for you?
My love is safe and true.

Don't be afraid
I know your frame and how you are made
I created you to truly know Me
My ways, character, heart, love and grace.

Words are not enough for you I know
So My good deeds to you I will always show.

Been told life has no meaning, no reason to be here?
That is so untrue, such lies, these I despise.

You are Mine, no-one can snatch you from My hand.

You were not a mistake, you were born of Me
Not of human will or descent.

You belong to Me.

Written when I moved into my new home with only a camping chair.

Notes

The Courts of Heaven

I write about this subject because it is a reality. Two years ago, I heard about it and was told to read a book called 'Accessing the Courts of Heaven' by Robert Henderson.[4] It was out of stock, so I asked questions to friends who I trust. They told me a few scriptures which I kind of just took as true, but I did no real study on the subject. Once, at our home church meeting, a lady wanted us to pray for her. The leader invited us all to enter a court in heaven to hear her case. When I was there, I saw Jesus as the Defence Advocate with the Father as the Judge sitting on a big seat (a throne) and all the angels listening, some whose jobs were to scribe every word that was going to be spoken that day. The other main person in there was the Accuser. He had papers to bring to the Judge to condemn the Defendant, who was the lady asking for prayer. I was stunned. I saw the Accuser telling the Judge what she had done wrong, breaking God's law deserving to be punished. Jesus the Defence Advocate was eager to forgive her, He really wanted to. He took the punishment for us all. What she needed to do was to confess this. I

---

[4] Robert Henderson, *Accessing the Courts of Heaven: Positioning yourself for Breakthrough and Answered Prayers* (Shippensburg, Pennsylvania: Destiny Image Publishers, 2017)

and others had words of knowledge for her about specific wrongs she had done recently. We told her and she confessed to them and asked for forgiveness. Jesus forgave her, so the charge was dropped, and she was free to leave the court a forgiven, free woman. The Accuser had no leg to stand on. However, because he is a legalist he will keep accusing you to the Judge who is totally righteous. Justice must be served. Jesus fulfilled every legal requirement for us to be free from guilt and condemnation! (Isaiah 53)

I was truly amazed at the love and mercy from the court.

Romans 7:6 is about the Law, it says "But now we have been released from the Law *and* its penalty, having died [through Christ] to that by which we were held captive." So if you read through Romans chapter 7, you will understand this.

"Therefore there is now NO condemnation for those in Christ Jesus!" (Romans 8:1 NIV)

When we judge others, we are in fact judging ourselves.

"Therefore you have no excuse *or* justification, everyone of you who [hypocritically] judges *and* condemns others; for in passing judgment on another person, you condemn yourself, because you who judge [from a position of arrogance or self-righteousness] are *habitually* practicing the very same things [which you denounce]." (Romans 2:1)

Please try not to do it. There is a law operating here, it is righteous. The Judge is our loving, perfect Father, who has provided for ALL our redemption by sending His Son to die for our sins. "For our sake He made Christ [virtually] to be sin Who knew no sin, so that in *and* through Him we might become [endued with, viewed as being in, and examples of] the righteousness of God [what we ought to be, approved and acceptable and in right relationship with Him, by His goodness]" (2 Corinthians 5:21)

The Court of Heaven I went to

A few months ago, I was waiting to have an appointment for some healing with a few trusted ministers who I know quite well. One night, a few days before the appointment, I lay in my bed and then in the Spirit I was in an office next door to a court. I saw loads of books and archives on shelves there with names on. I saw my file, a book of life on a shelf with my name on it. It was thick and heavy as I picked it up. Inside was every single word that had been spoken to me by every single person in my life. At significant, painful times in my life there was a red stamp at the bottom right-hand corner of those pages, saying in capital red letters "REPAYMENT DUE". I knew this was the Lord speaking to me. I realised the scripture "I will repay you for the years the locusts have eaten." (Joel 2:25 NIV) was true. I was very excited and became expectant of this and many more promises He has given me.

A few days later, again in my bed, I saw lots of angels in a court who were talking to each other. I knew they were the ones who were going to be with me at my trial and to witness my case at my appointment. I was amazed. I managed to write down a few of the scriptures that they were reading. The Lord said to me that the angels will concur on these things. I saw them nodding and confidently smiling at each other.

At my appointment, I was confessing and repenting of all the sins, transgressions and iniquities the Lord was revealing to me. This meant I could go to the court and not have to be accused of anything as I was declared free because of my repentance. The Accuser had nothing on me. He was silenced. Jesus my Defence Advocate won the case, the Righteous Judge, our Father declared His judgement that I was free from condemnation and punishment. I walked free. The angels were there too, rejoicing alongside the witnesses in the room with me.

This appointment was to be followed by another one a few weeks later.

The Court of Heaven where I came out with my goods

In this appointment, I went, in the Spirit, to a court with the ladies who were praying for me again as they are more experienced than me in these matters. I trusted them to help and guide me. We were not exactly sure where to go, so we asked at reception. The lady there passed on our information to the court and we had to sit in a waiting room. Several minutes later, a big, strong, handsome angel carried out with him a massive sack full of treasures. These were the things stolen from me. They had been reclaimed. At a court there is a place where stolen goods are retrieved and returned to owners, and this was exactly what was happening for me. The sack was so big I needed assistance to carry it, so my friends helped me. I could not take all of this in, it was mind-blowing but true. I realised that as there was so much treasure it would take time to sort through. So, I was given a safe to put things in. Only I knew the secret code to open and close it. No one else was allowed access to it unless with my consent.

Notes

The Retrieved Treasures

I am still looking at, touching, enjoying and considering these treasures. Every day I am waking up receiving love, affirmation, hope and joy never experienced before. I know this will continue and increase, it is certainly eternal! Sometimes when I am overwhelmed with peace, I ask the Lord what is going on as it often happens unexpectedly. He says to me "And this, Antoinette is the repayment." My family are beginning to get reconciled which is really completely orchestrated by the Lord otherwise there would have been no chance. My siblings and I are spending time together; we all realise that we need to do this because we were separated through our childhoods. We are all thinking, independently of each other, the very same things. It is amazing, I am thanking God for this. New revelations about our family are coming to light too. I am delighted. The Lord keeps saying the same thing. "And this, Antoinette is the repayment." I know there is much more to come, as there are more treasures in my safe to enjoy and give away.

We may have forgotten about life's painful trials and tribulations but our Father has not. His desire is to repay each one of us according to His unfailing love, justice, kindness and goodness. NEVER, ever forget you are incredibly unique, you never have to compare your life with anyone else's. He longs to do you good. He understands how and when to bring you the personal revelation of who He is and who you are in Him. He is your best friend too, you can always rely on Him. He wants all of you, because He loves every bit of you and will do so forever!

"Now to Him Who, by (in consequence of) the [action of His] power that is at work within us, is able to [carry out His purpose and] do superabundantly, far over *and* above all that we [dare] ask or think [infinitely beyond our highest prayers, desires, thoughts, hopes, or dreams]– [21] To Him be glory in the church and in Christ Jesus throughout all generations forever and ever. Amen (so be it)." (Ephesians 3:20-21)

Notes

The Waiting Room in the Court

One evening recently, only a few weeks ago I was lying on my bed talking to the Lord. I knew there was an office in heaven where our ministry is based as well as on the earth. I thought I should be able to go there to see it as it is.

Immediately I walked through a glass door. I saw a waiting area, it was calm, peaceful, full of love, clean and pristine throughout. No stress at all. There were desks, chairs, tables and armchairs. It was so warm and welcoming. We were met by angels, all wearing smart suits in different colours, who treated us with utmost respect and honour. We were there to see how our cases were progressing and what was happening with them. There was even a sideboard and a table with coffee, tea and all sorts of expensive cakes for us to enjoy.

"Thank you for your patience in waiting," said an angel. "All your cases and petitions have been heard, seen and read. They are all in hand, being processed, your wait is because they are being thoroughly sorted, each one to the letter."

To one who was unsure if their case was important or significant, he said "Your case is not unimportant or insignificant to the court and it has been heard."

The angels were chatting to us, reassuring us and encouraging us and were there to answer any questions we had or to advise us regarding our cases. We all had one to talk to personally.

There were some who were not quite sure what to do and how to do it regarding their cases that they wanted to bring to the court. Their angels explained their rights to them and gave them options and choices of how to go about the things concerning them. They were also given a leaflet called 'YOUR RIGHTS,' which described what you can do because of what Jesus did at the cross, to take home, read and decide a plan of action to put further cases forward, with personal options and choices.

Others were given a list of specific instructions, things to do and say when they got home. Others were given writs.

Definition of a Writ: A formal written, authoritative command. These writs were also specific and personal.

A beautiful, strong, old, lady angel, who carried authority and who was fully knowledgeable and experienced in the court proceedings and practices smiled at us and said, "He is good you know, He is the best. He has never lost a case, He always wins!"

The angels smiled, then said the same thing to each other, nodded their heads and concurred together. Then they smiled at us saying the same thing. "He is good you know, He is the best. He has never lost a case. He always wins!"

Their eyes were beautiful, shining and full of love. There was so much love, peace, companionship and family love shared between us all.

I did not want to leave.

Notes

A Biblical View of the Courts of Heaven

Here are a few main scriptures to support this topic. I know these to be true, alongside many who have helped minister to people and have witnessed and observed what is happening in the courts of heaven during this process. They have been given revelation, helping them to see defendants walk free from the court with no punishment for their wrongdoings, or for the consequences of breaking God's law.

Luke 18 is about a woman who kept asking the judge to grant her justice against her adversary. Jesus said to listen to what the unjust judge says, then He talked of how the Just Judge, who is our Father, will respond to our requests.

"Come to terms quickly with your accuser while you are on your way travelling with him to court; lest your accuser hand you over to the judge, and the judge to the guard, and you be put in prison." (Matthew 5:25) Your accuser is Satan.

"Put Me in remembrance [remind Me of your merits]; let us plead *and* argue together. Set forth your case, that you may be justified (proved right)." (Isaiah 43:26)

God tells us to bring our cases to Him.

God is a Righteous Judge. (Psalm 7:11)

He is our Advocate, "Therefore, since we have a great high priest who has ascended into heaven, Jesus the Son of God, let us hold firmly to the faith we profess. For we do not have a high priest who is unable to empathize with our weaknesses, but we have one who has been tempted in every way, just as we are—yet he did not sin. Let us then approach God's throne of grace with confidence, so that we may receive mercy and find grace to help us in our time of need." (Hebrews 4:14-16 NIV)

"But He holds His priesthood unchangeably, because He lives on forever. Therefore He is able also to save to the uttermost (completely, perfectly, finally, and for all time and eternity) those who come to God through Him, since He is always living to make petition to God *and* intercede with Him *and* intervene for them." (Hebrews 7:24-25)

"Christ the Messiah is therefore the Negotiator and Mediator of an [entirely] new agreement." (Hebrews 9:15)

"Do not fret or have anxiety about anything, but in every circumstance *and* in everything, by prayer and petition (definite requests), with thanksgiving, continue to make your wants known to God. (Philippians 4:6)

Definition of Solicit: Seek to obtain by asking for.

Solicitation: appeal for, ask for, beg, beseech, entreat, petition, request, importune.

Definition of Importunate: making persistent requests.

Jesus is our Solicitor!

"Only One is the Lawgiver *and* Judge Who is able to save and destroy." (James 4:12)

We are also told that we will refute every tongue that condemns us:

"No weapon turned against you will succeed. You will silence every voice raised up to accuse you. These benefits are enjoyed by the servants of the LORD; their vindication will come from Me. I, the LORD, have spoken." (Isaiah 54:17 NLT)

This is what we are to do in the court, to keep agreeing with Jesus.

Definition of Vindicate: Clear of blame, justify. Absolve, prove, support.

Can you see these words are used in the Judicial System too?

I recommend a further study of this subject. It is full of revelation from the Lord.

As a teenager I watched a programme called 'Crown Court.' I loved to hear the arguments between the Defence and Prosecution. The evidence is always based on facts. The Law is always fundamental in every case heard. It is always upheld and, after hearing cases for both the Defence and the Prosecution, the Judge makes the final decision about the punishment that the defendant gets if he or she is found guilty of the charges against him or her. The Judge is the one who has the final say because he has ultimate authority.

Remember, our punishment was upon Jesus, so we can have peace, freedom from condemnation. All we have to do is to confess our wrongdoings, confess breaking God's laws, receive forgiveness, break ancestral ties, forgive those who have hurt us and repent, which means to turn away from.

The Holy Spirit will reveal these things to us; we can indeed walk free from every consequence of sin, transgression and iniquity in our lives and be in a perfect, unbreakable relationship with our Perfect Father, Jesus and the Holy Spirit forever. Yes, you will continue to sin and iniquity and transgression will be operating; He will free you from it over time as and when He reveals these things personally to you.

"If we say we have no sin [refusing to admit that we are sinners], we delude *and* lead ourselves astray, and the Truth [which the Gospel presents] is not in us [does not dwell in our hearts]. If we [freely] admit that we have sinned *and* confess our sins, He is faithful and just (true to His own nature and promises) and will forgive our sins [dismiss our lawlessness] and [continuously] cleanse us from all unrighteousness [everything not in conformity to His will in purpose, thought, and action]. If we say (claim) we have not sinned, we contradict His Word *and* make Him out to be false *and* a liar, and His Word is not in us [the divine message of the Gospel is not in our hearts]." (1 John 1:8-10)

"He who conceals his transgressions will not prosper; whoever confesses and turns away from his sins will find compassion *and* mercy." (Proverbs 28:13)

I love that our God always speaks the truth. He is always right and merciful.

A POEM

You Belong to Me

You belong to Me
Your sin, transgressions and iniquities are sorted
My plans will not be aborted
I am with you, you're not alone but escorted.

Every cell in your body was uniquely made
The price of redemption, total healing has been paid
Wholeness is yours!
It is intimate, the best
Where you are fulfilled and at complete rest!

God already knows what the things are that hinder our relationship with Him.

A few more words to encourage you:
Despite the sin and iniquity within, I covered you and will continue to do so. In your mother's womb you were under the shadow of My wing. You are still there as I have always encompassed your life and always will, all around your life, every single area of it.

The Types of Courts of Heaven

For further study of this subject, I recommend Robert Henderson's book, 'Accessing the Courts of Heaven.' [5]

I also recommend the following Bible passages, reflecting these topics:

The Court of Mediation / Reconciliation.... 2 Corinthians 5:13

The Throne of Grace... Hebrews 4:6

The Court of Mount Zion.... Hebrews 12:22-24

The Court of the Accuser.... Revelation 12:10

The Court of the Ancient of Days (The Supreme Court)... Daniel 17:9

The Lord will teach you how they work, their functions, operations and purpose, and His in them. You will be blessed!

I trust you will be able to discover and recover, recover and discover, discover and recover ALL that is rightfully yours, appropriating everything that has been done for you by Jesus Christ. I trust this will also be one of your many answered prayers.

---

[5] Robert Henderson, *Accessing the Courts of Heaven: Positioning yourself for Breakthrough and Answered Prayers* (Shippensburg, Pennsylvania: Destiny Image Publishers, 2017)

Notes

Rebuilding Your Life

Our lives are built on what we believe about ourselves. Each thing we accept as being part of our makeup could be called a single brick. Every single one is made up of our views, memories, actions and life experiences and determines how we live.

To rebuild our lives there are bricks which need to be thrown away, such as false hope, false guilt, fears, accepting abuse, feeling we do not have any choices, having false obligations towards others, being easily manipulated, programmed, never questioning, just agreeing with everything, being silenced, inferiority and other negative things in our lives. Our lives need rebuilding with good, holy, strong, believing, positive, faith filled bricks which the Lord will cement in our inmost beings.

Here are a few things I wrote, my good bricks which are now new ones cemented in. I realised that personal choice is ALWAYS mine, then I gave myself permission to walk away from abusive behaviour towards me, because God gives me permission to do so.

I now refuse to be manipulated by anyone.

I am not responsible for others' bad behaviour.

I will not put my trust in people or anything else except the Lord.

I cannot save anyone, only God can do that.

I do not have to agree with everything others say or do.

I do not need to rely on others hearing from the Lord for me because I know His voice for myself. I can hear Him because I am His daughter.

I came to these conclusions over a period of time, a process of being healed, and becoming strong enough to carry the new bricks inside me.

Ask the Holy Spirit to reveal to you what bricks need to be thrown out, these bricks will be replaced with new bricks placed, built in, cemented in perfectly by Him and will strengthen and enhance your life. You will be more whole, more like Jesus.

At times we feel like our lives are falling apart; the reality is they are being rebuilt. Remember, God wants to restore you back to His original design and state before sin came into the world.

Removing the Residue of Religion

Recently, the Lord said to me that He is removing the residue of religion in His people. I saw a pink plastic bucket with a thin murky layer of religious residue at the bottom of it. We have all been subjected to this in church because it is always there operating. We rarely complain about it, even though we are aware of it. It is a spiritual enemy damaging our very beings. It can cause inferiority, stunt our level of spiritual growth and put barriers in front of us to succeed spiritually. It can also cause competitiveness, jealousy, and all the things that are common divisive methods that our enemy uses to destroy each and every one of us. Remember, the church is a body, we all need each other to function effectively. We are commanded to love each other, bear with each other and be gentle. Read Colossians chapter 3.

Our wonderful Father desires to remove this residue for us. He will reveal aspects of it to us as we let Him change us. We only need to ask. We are being changed all the time as we go through the process of sanctification.

"Now may the God of peace Himself sanctify you through and through [that is, separate you from profane and vulgar things, make you pure and whole and undamaged—consecrated to Him—set apart for His purpose]; and may your spirit and soul and body be kept complete and [be found] blameless at the coming of our Lord Jesus Christ. Faithful *and* absolutely trustworthy is He who is calling you [to Himself for your salvation], and He will do it [He will fulfill His call by making you holy, guarding you, watching over you, and protecting you as His own]." (1 Thessalonians 5:23)

He knows that activities we do which are not led by the Holy Spirit can wear us out and make us carry false responsibilities, which cause us to feel burdened. However, His yoke is easy and His burden is light.

"Come to Me, all you who labour and are heavy-laden *and* overburdened, and I will cause you to rest. [I will ease and relieve and refresh your souls.] Take My yoke upon you and learn of Me, for I am gentle (meek) and humble (lowly) in heart, and you will find rest (relief and ease and refreshment and recreation and blessed quiet) for your souls. For My yoke is wholesome (useful, good—not harsh, hard, sharp, or pressing, but comfortable, gracious, and pleasant), and My burden is light *and* easy to be borne." (Matthew 11:28-30)

"In fact, this is love for God: to keep his commands. And his commands are not burdensome," (1 John 5:3)

We are all influenced by doctrines in our churches, they usually determine our actions.

Definition of Doctrine: Principles of a religious, political, or other group.

Doctrinal: Belief, conviction, creed, dogma, precept, principle, tenet.

An example of this is saying the Creed in church, assuming that this is necessary to access God. This constitutes an unnecessary religious activity.

Praying for someone you meet daily is another one. Not necessary.

Giving to your church's chosen mission is another. You feel an ungodly obligation to do so though.

Believing that God only speaks through the Bible or creation is another one.

Believing that it is only the Pastor who can give out the bread and wine for communion.

Thinking that Youth Workers need to be under 30 years old.

The use of objects in worship, e.g. incense burners, candles, crosses or images in church.

Focussing on controversial issues, e.g. the perfect Bible translation or age at which children should or not be baptised and how deep should the water be.

Going along with what everyone thinks is important, e.g. having a drop-in centre in the church for use in the community.

Having to have fresh flowers in church.

Believing that only the leaders can prophesy in church.

Believing that you have to go to a home group once a week.

Agreeing with the details of a vision of the local church even if you don't.

Feeling obligated to attend certain conferences, ladies or men's groups.

Feeling obligated to contribute to a discussion during a Bible study.

Feeling like your value is based on the things you do in church.

There are others too, alongside traditions we follow.

Definition of a Tradition: Conventional, customary, established, habitual, normal, regular, routine, time-honoured and usual.

Jesus kept all the Jewish feasts. In John 7, He celebrated the Feast of Tabernacles. Mark's gospel, chapter 7 is about how the disciples were eating with unwashed hands; see Jesus' response to the Pharisees' complaints to Him. Traditions can become more important than

God's laws. Remember God's laws are always based on love, the wellbeing and dignity of humanity. Matthew 12 is about the Pharisees complaining that the disciples were doing what was unlawful on the Sabbath by eating grains in a field because they were hungry. Hear and consider Jesus' response to this.

"Religion that God our Father accepts as PURE and faultless is this; to look after orphans and widows in their distress and keep oneself from being polluted by the world." (James 1:27 NIV)

The use of the word PURE implies that there can be impurity.

This is a chapter which, if we really want to be more like Jesus, will challenge us a lot. Most religious residue is hidden. We need the Holy Spirit to reveal truth to us, so we can be fully free and cleansed from it. This will leave more room for the Lord to fill us with Himself.

"Behold, You desire truth in the innermost being, And in the hidden part [of my heart] You will make me know wisdom." (Psalm 51:6)

"Search me, O God, and know my heart; test me and know my anxious thoughts. Point out anything in me that offends you, and lead me along the path of everlasting life." (Psalm 139:23-24 NLT)

The Lord delights in your responses to Him. He really wants a close, personal, intimate relationship with you because He loves you forever and knows your response at this very moment. Nothing can or will separate you from His love!

Read Romans 8:35 to the end.

He will convince you of this too!

You Were Made for Much More than the Ordinary!

Each and every one of us has a calling from the Lord, it is perfect for each of us to live out, truly being ourselves, living in the freedom that Jesus has made possible. This is a life which is supernatural, exciting, which has to be fought for, taking us out of our comfort zones and out of human reasoning. A life less than this can seem meaningless, unfruitful, monotonous and boring. You were made for much more than the ordinary, you are a spiritual and natural being designed to work with the Lord, in Christ and with angelic beings in heavenly realms which are high above our earthly ones.

Are you living life to the full?

Jesus said, "I came that you might have and enjoy life *and* have it in abundance [to the full till it overflows]." (John 10:10)

You are getting there, as you discover and recover more of what is already yours. The process, however challenging it can be, is worth it. You are authentic, unique, sincere and true, called by Him... intimately and personally.

Thank you for reading this. After 34 years of waiting, I have found one of my purposes is to write this book. I am overwhelmed with how this has become a reality. I have written poetry for years, sharing only with a few close friends recently. I have just gone for it and obeyed the Lord.

Do whatever He tells you, find brothers and sisters who you can trust, who love you, this will ultimately lead to fullness of life!

The LORD will fulfil His purpose for your life, He will perfect that which concerns you. "The LORD will accomplish that which concerns me; Your [unwavering] lovingkindness, O LORD, endures forever—Do not abandon the works of Your own hands." (Psalm 138:8)

Love and blessings,

Antoinette Murphy.

As you continue in the process of discovering and recovering, you will find that trades will be made:

Trades will be made
Giants in your life will be slayed
Memories will fade.

You will be repaid
Walk confidently in the promises He has made.

In your life, His glory will be displayed
You will be glad you persevered, trusted and stayed.

Your confidence will grow
You will not be so afraid

You will be fulfilled, blessed and truly satisfied
Be able to live your life in Him, not having to hide.

Notes